Zack's House

by
Laurel Dickey

Pioneer Valley Educational Press, Inc.

"Mom, can you play with me?" said Zack.

Mom said, "No, I can not play. I'm too busy."

Zack sat under the table.
"This is my house," he said.

Zack got pillows and a rug.
Then he put a blanket on the table.

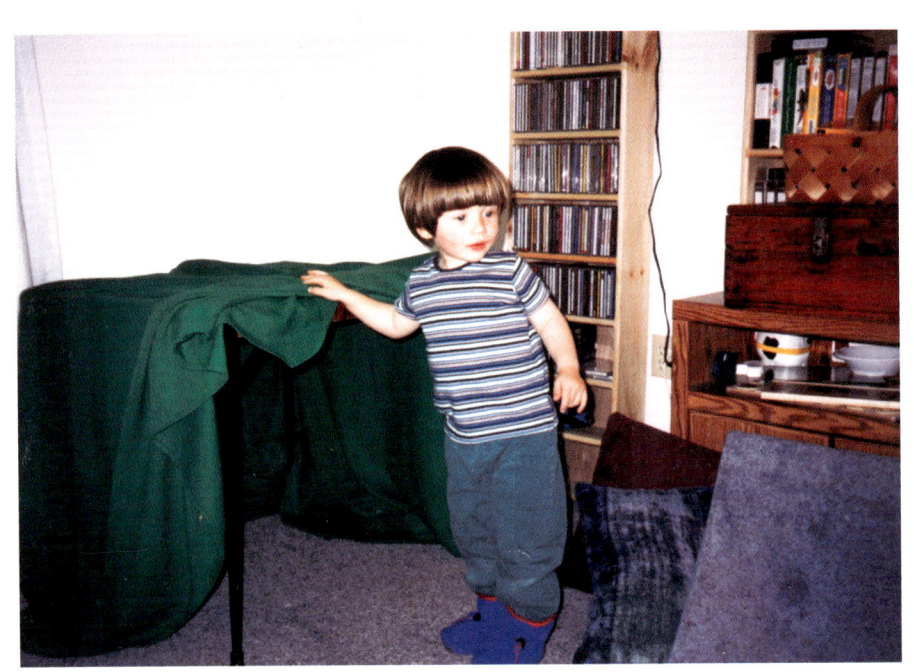

Zack put the pillows in the house.
He put the rug in the house, too.

"Look, Mom," said Zack.
"I made a house!
I can go in my house."

"I like your house. Can I come in and play?" said Mom. "I'm not too busy to play, now."

Zack and Mom played in the house all day.
"I like my house," said Zack.

"Yes," said Mom.
"You made a good house!"